LIFTING THE SKY

Lifting the Sky

Southwestern Haiku & Haiga

Poetry of the American Southwest — No. 1

**Edited by Scott Wiggerman
& Constance Campbell**

Foreword by Penny Harter

Dos Gatos Press
Austin, Texas

Lifting the Sky:
Southwestern Haiku and Haiga
© 2013 , Dos Gatos Press
ISBN13: 978–09840399–3–7
Library of Congress Control Number: 2013937148

Lifting the Sky is the first in a new series from Dos Gatos Press: Poetry of the American Southwest.

First Edition:
13 14 15 16 17 18 5 4 3 2 1

Cover Photograph:
"Red Door" by Carol King — ckinggalleries.com

Cover Design: David Meischen and Scott Wiggerman

Chapter Division Page Photographs: David Meischen

Manufacturing: OneTouchPoint Ginny's

Dos Gatos Press
1310 Crestwood Rd.
Austin, TX 78722
www.dosgatospress.org

Contents

FOREWORD

I am honored to have been asked to write the foreword to this luminous anthology of haiku and haiga reflecting the four seasons in the American Southwest . My late husband, William J. (Bill) Higginson, and I moved to Santa Fe in 1991, and we hadn't been there long before I announced to him, "This is the place where air is made." The mountains seemed part of the sky, and the Milky Way had never looked so clear. The title of this volume also calls us into the sky, as does the title poem by Lesley Anne Swanson:

> lifting the sky
> high over Arizona
> saguaro arms

During our eleven years living in Santa Fe, Bill and I traveled throughout New Mexico, as well as into Colorado, West Texas (where my parents had relocated from New Jersey), and California. Since then I have visited my sister in the Texas Hill Country. Although New Mexico is often referred to as the Land of Enchantment, the whole region enchants me.

If I were writing a review of this volume, I'd find it hard to stop quoting poems, and I'd want to find a way to reproduce many of the wonderful haiga that are so aptly placed within the overall flow of the work. It's clear that the editors deeply cared about the ongoing order of the poems, both within the seasonal sections (starting with Fall) and within the book as a whole.

Here we enter haiku and haiga that take us through the beauties of the landscape — from desert and mountains to the sea; poems that express the poets' political, spiritual, mythical, cultural, and deeply personal connections to the Southwest; poems that make us laugh or cry; and poems drenched in light that repeatedly carry us from the Earth into the stars and galaxies. As does the landscape, these poems lift us out of ourselves. And this is underscored in the closing haiga, by Allene Rasmussen Nichols:

> all things vanish here —
> horned lizards, animal bones
> cactus blooms
> and
> us

Back in 1992, shortly after Bill and I had moved to Santa Fe, I wrote the following haiku:

> a morning glory
> cupped in his hand —
> the sky

This anthology is like that morning glory. Cradle it, open it, and enjoy!

Penny Harter

March 2013

秋

Fall

early autumn
each leaf
on a journey
~ Máire Morrissey-Cummins

a thin shining line
cast by a spider —
October morning
~ Sandra D. Lynn

blue norther
a mosquito
clings to the door
~ Shannon Dougherty

rosy twilight
creeps up the mountain —
Taos sunset
~ Charlie Rossiter

autumn mist slithers
between Chisos peaks,
coils around rock
~ Barbara Blake

school bus stop
papí hugs goodbye
in English
~ Roberta Beary

broken-winged magpie
hops ahead of me
~ Jane DeJonghe

sunset
two old people
watch the waves
~ Joanna M. Weston

rain
the patter of piñones
on two gray hills
~ Lesley Anne Swanson

first frost
wild Turk's cap
tamed
~ Mary F. Whiteside

red sand hills
the shape of hornos
I unfold my easel
~ Neal Whitman

ocotillo displays
parched leaves — no flowers
bare branches beg for alms

~ Christine Wenk-Harrison

koi swim
among falling autumn leaves
red, orange, gold
~ Frances Briggs

fierce sun beats down
Texas thirst meets iced
Oktoberfest beer
~ Sue Foster

turning to fire the trees the earth
~ Mark E. Brager

on a walking trail
in the Blue Mountains —
parrot feathers, dry leaves
~ Lisa Hase-Jackson

aimless wandering
I catch the day moon
winking at me
~ Robert Epstein

high desert scrub oak
rattles October breeze
red leaves clinging to life

~ Jerry Hamby

a child running
through dried milkweed —
seeds given wings

~ Lillian Susan Thomas

autumn wind
blasts through all the cracks
in my composure
~ Joe Blanda

October blues
cry of a piñon jay
from the feeder
~ Charles Trumbull

buffalos at rest
in a sea of sandy wheat
boulders in the waves
~ Sally Clark

red cliff face
brims with pictographs
handprints like mine
~ Doris Lynch

Mother asked for rain.
Daughter asked for snow.
Father asked for *son*.
~ Jennifer Smith

8

prairie fire . . .

mdornaus

the smoldering echo
of forgotten songs

~ Margaret Dornaus

feather in the grass
now that summer's flight is done
will you write for me

~ Aletha Irby

first frost —
icy vines
with one red tomato

~ Chris Ellery

snow-on-the-prairie
scatters winter white
among fallen leaves

~ Linda Banks

trophy-wall trout —
his final leap
into sunlight

~ p. wick

alone on a park bench:
the song of the sparrow
reminds me of her

~ Stephen Page

Veterans Day
a stranger gives me
the peace sign

~ Joan Prefontaine

leaf-clotted gutters
spilling soured rain
and you say, don't grieve

~ Christine Boldt

clouds so low
I'm walking
through them

~ Jane De Jonghe

tall grass
I reach for your hand
without asking

~ Margaret Dornaus

piñon gathering
how sticky
the scent of pine

~ Doris Lynch

empty gate
I enter the way
of the butterfly

~ Robert Epstein

stooping to gather
maple leaves, I become
a child again
~ Sandra Cobb

tufts of rabbitbrush —
coyote waits
beside a shaft of moonlight
~ Lesley Anne Swanson

Bastrop pines
old reflections
lost

~ Amy Greenspan

this fall's leaves
drifting to rest
in last year's
~ Shannon Dougherty

fat raindrops
raise puffs of dust
the scent of sage
~ Ellaraine Lockie

with new appetites
eager hands strip the earth
racing toward sunset
~ Dayna Bradley

autumn sun on cypress
hill country river
reflecting copper
~ Amy Greenspan

narrow road
headlights search the canyon walls
starlit stone
~ Dennis Magliozzi

temperatures plunge
forty degrees in an hour —
Stetson tumbles south

~ Sylvia Riojas Vaughn

company —
the first leaf takes a seat
near me on the bank

~ Vasile Moldovan

Shiner Bocks
and sherry-splashed mushrooms
tapas with mi tía

~ Peg Duthie

the smell of morning
sits on the kitchen table
beside the pepper

~ Loretta Diane Walker

Walmart parking lot
a thousand grackles converge
loud, rude, messy

~ Susan Beall Summers

crimson aspen leaf
or poison sumac?
I'm not touching that!

~ Wayne Lee

fence near bump gate
displays six coyote pelts —
fair warning

~ Ann Howells

September sunset
dead juniper
gleams copper

~ Sandra D. Lynn

16

dawn the chiaroscuro warmth of adobe
~ Sergio Ortiz

the weight
of all those stones
Labor Day

~ Joan Prefontaine

tequila dreams
the half-moon floating
in amber
~ Mark E. Brager

dark clouds fly
into luminous twilight
a thousand thousand bats
~ Geoffrey A. Landis

October's chilling dusk
a gray owl wakes
~ Evelyn Corry Appelbee

chamomile tea
I close my eyes to hear
the night bird
~ Sergio Ortiz

harvest-moon zephyr
wheels over canyon hoodoos
ghost-whistle
~ Jan Benson

late night cockroaches
visit sleeping library
consuming Kafka
~ John E. Rice

jack-o'-lantern's
innocent candle-lit grin —
strangers with candy
~ Jerri Hardesty

the wolves and I
howling at the moon
children of the night
~ Brenda Roberts

Roswell
searching the skies
a lightning flash
~ Cliff Roberts

nest of pecans
your brown fingers scrub
at the bitter skins

~ Peg Duthie

fog spirits away
the familiar — earth like me
longs to be alone
~ Aletha Irby

cloud shifts across
a September night sky —
the last moonflower
~ Scott Wiggerman

even the streetlights
glow with meaning —
autumn mist
~ Constance Campbell

el mundo tranquilo
entre temporadas
una pausa

the world quiet
between seasons
a pause
~ Becky Liestman

Winter

waiting for snowfall
in the closed window
a white geranium

~ Vasile Moldovan

first calligraphy —
a pine tree's shadow
on the snowy clearing

~ Vasile Moldovan

tiny feather
wind dances
across snow bank

~ Jane De Jonghe

silently he came
and silently departed
snow on the mountain

~ Richard Wells

silent flakes fall
wild turkey's red feet
crunch the snow's crust
~ Gretchen Fletcher

hoofprints lead deep
into the mesquite thicket —
snow on yuccas
~ J. Todd Hawkins

snowy field
winter pours
from the pinto's nostrils
~ Doris Lynch

remaining snow
a bald eagle soars
over the Rio Grande
~ Charles Trumbull

cactus owl retreats
deep into saguaro nest
snow dusts the yuccas
~ Ann Howells

yesterday
the ice castle
was an old shed
~ Linda Banks

crystal ice forest
in the midnight hush
leaves crackle, limbs pop
~ James Willard

blowing snow
my teacup warm
but empty

~ Pearl Pirie

rarest visitor
snowflakes dance their brief dance
on blue northern winds

~ Peter Holland

all morning
snow drifting over the trail —
your icy breath

~ Roy Beckemeyer

virgin snow
her wedding dress
of ivory lace

~ Máire Morrissey-Cummins

white parka
and red snow boots
winter roses

~ Joanna M. Weston

the farmhouse burns
ashes black against the snow
snake bones

~ Miranda Nicole

winter wind
slips through the corridor
chafing hands
~ Becky Liestman

the dunes shift
in their sleep
~ Shannon Dougherty

a flight of gulls framed
by waves and low winter clouds
in what frame am I

~ Larry Kelly

faded sofa
the old cat purrs
no comforter required

~ p. wick

December sun
rattlesnake suddenly
has something to say

~ Joan Prefontaine

ravens on white cliffs
sun warming their wings
we gather firewood

~ Darla McBryde

bare black branches
then the owl's voice

~ Cindy Huyser

vultures circle wide
keen eyes focused below —
border patrol

~ Christine Wenk-Harrison

fragile feather beats
against an adobe wall
driven by the wind

~ Gretchen Fletcher

bosque quietude
one shrike in silhouette
dusk in the pines

~ Neal Whitman

*rusty windmill clanks
in December's wind, a song
of thirsty birds*

~ Cindy Huyser

seasonless city
brown wren nests in door wreath
Christmas comes early

~ Carolyn Dahl

sleigh bells jingle
on a grass-bound sled —
Christmas in Texas

~ Jan Benson

Texas Christmas
snow melts before
the last present

~ Cliff Roberts

winter sunlight
our neighbors bring us
homemade tamales

~ Lynn Edge

Christmas morning
twenty stockings hang
empty

~ Susan Beall Summers

Mamá's gifts
filled, wrapped, tied with care —
tamales

~ Christine Wenk-Harrison

Christmas Day
unopened gifts
tell the story

~ Barbara Green Powell

Christmas weekend,
plaza bums
beg for coins

~ Charlie Kossiter

luminarias
line casita rooftops
who cares about stars?

~ Doris Lynch

clouds smudge
a charcoal sky —
winter solstice

~ Sandra Cobb

Orion hunts the night sky
how far light must travel

~ Sandi Stromberg

winter sunset
on the desert
all in red

~ Joseph Stack

winter sunset . . .
mother's blue eyes
search the horizon

~ Margaret Dornaus

faint and fickle
sliding in with slanted eyes
January light

~ Susan Gabrielle

no one remembers
if the last sunset on earth
took our breath away

~ Albert Vetere Lannon
~ Artwork by Kaitlin Mara Meadows

seventy-fifth year
the winter moon and I
still dream
~ Mel Goldberg

against moonglow
one ant on a blade of grass
shivering
~ Marcelle Kasprowicz

white and honest moon
reflected in bath water
I will meet my life
~ Elizabeth Jacobson

distant train whistle:
the moon
sails undisturbed
~ Geoffrey A. Landis

panhandle moon
we follow the snow geese home
empty-handed
~ Margaret Dornaus

frost settles white
on ristras — colder still
the gibbous moon
~ Lisa Hase-Jackson

moon deepens the well
as rainfall tapers off . . .
faint sense of myself
~ Rebecca Lilly

if the heart takes time
then take it under these stars —
this moon slicing white
~ Mike Burwell

what's left of the moon —
a slice — ripe cantaloupe — set
on a chilled glass plate
~ Robert A. Ayres

storm clouds . . .
a small circle of stones
in the dry earth
~ Mark E. Brager

hospice vigil —
the week-old roses
scent our whispers
~ Rebecca Lilly

news of his death
the passing shadows
of crows
~ Máire Morrissey-Cummins

bone-chilling rain
some hurts
you can't shake off
~ Robert Epstein

bone-cold winter
bare branches against gray skies
cat under the stove
~ Ron Blanton

in my rain gutters
chips of the oak tree cut down
for a swimming pool

~ Larry Kelly
~ Artwork by Danny Clark

quiet house hums
all winter the pellet stove
spits and grinds

~ Lori Desrosiers

the cold wind
and the old men's hot air —
country store

~ Brenda Roberts

reading
old love letters
scent of winter

~ Máire Morrissey-Cummins

old wooden stairs and knees
creak in the cold —
another year ends

~ Meloni Davis

seven thousand feet
at the Kachina Lodge
oxygen bar

~ Ellaraine Lockie

cliffside veined with ice
the sun's too pale to melt
this New Year's morning
~ Joseph Hutchison

ground stone and marrow on canyon wall
for four thousand years
I lived

~ Gloria Amescua

hungry doves
beg at the empty feeder
winter morning

~ Carolyn Tourney Florek

mean air
needles on skin
I weave, I weave

~ Cara Fox

lean winter
he is sure she will
make the trade with him

~ Jennifer Smith

through desert dusk
big rigs rolling toward Phoenix
lean coyotes watch

~ Alan Gann

hunger in the air
a lone coyote close . . .
closer

~ Evelyn Corry Appelbee

anticipation:
old men pot narcissus bulbs
remembering spring
~ John E. Rice

the pear tree's
hesitant buds —
February
~ Sally Clark

storm clouds
slashed and gaping   make a waterfall of sunshine
~ Meloni Davis

春

Spring

Kokopelli breathes
low notes on the flute —
spring wind

~ Lesley Anne Swanson

ocotillo red
only in springtime
she dresses wildly

~ Joan Prefontaine

spring gardening
my shoes
laced in cobwebs

~ Máire Morrissey-Cummins

tulips bloom
in a palette of colors —
winter's canvas ends

~ Sheri Sutton

blue juniper bush
springs from a bed of red rocks
keeping its foothold

~ Gretchen Fletcher

Oklahoma spring
flowering redbud
lighting my way

~ Margaret Dornaus

setting fires
on the bluebonnet hills:
Indian paintbrush

~ Lillian Susan Thomas

early spring hike
through freshly fallen snow —
a single violet bloom

~ James Willard

waiting for tulips
in a chill mountain valley
takes years of Aprils

~ Teresa Milbrodt

48

haiku day
a butterfly's shadow
flits through mine
  ~ Cliff Roberts

tight buds hold their blooms
rebirth at a snail's pace
no rush — mañana

~ Christine Wenk-Harrison

lantana buzzing
monarchs, longwings, skippers —
which one's on my cheek?

~ Cindy Huyser

Texas spring
the lawn mower buried
in bluebonnets

~ Cliff Roberts

white yucca flowers
in country cemetery
ghosts in the graveyard

~ Catherine L'Herisson

cemetery visit
the forget-me-nots
at home

~ Robert Epstein

only the dove's call
in the rural cemetery —
Memorial Day

~ Charles Trumbull

en la boca cerrada
no entran
flores de cereza

if you keep your mouth shut
they won't fall in —
cherry blossoms
~ Charles Trumbull

feathery faces

soaked in sun to blushing pink
night will cool them down

~ Christa Pandey

conifers still in snow
the canyon wren
looking down valley

~ p. wick

below the peach tree
flipping pages in a book
hummingbird flutter

~ Ellaraine Lockie

a finch sings
sweet and sour candy for the ear

~ Marcelle Kasprowicz

that sound you heard
a bird's wing in flight
whispering secrets

~ Jesse Castro

creek at sunset
mockingbird quilts
a tune

~ Shannon Dougherty

cold is memory
and I am seventy-five
still warm   still breathing
~ Albert Vetere Lannon

across asphalt
truck tires scatter grit
and white pear blossoms
~ Sandra D. Lynn

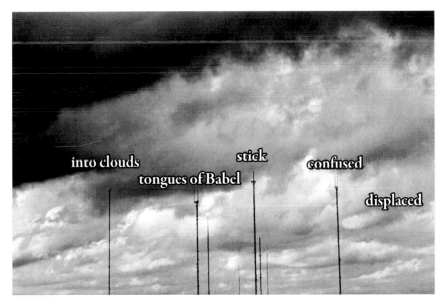

~ Wade Martin
~ Photograph by Katie Goode

mice scurry
across holy dirt
Chimayo pilgrims
~ Darla McBryde

squirrel shadow
tail a flickering question —
what next?
~ Gloria Amescua

field trip
the young snake
out-slithers me
~ Ann Spiers

cottontail
in the shade of mesquite
waits   waits   runs
~ Joy Acey

stagnant shadows
in bright desert noon
lizard dreams
~ Susan Beall Summers

small speckled gecko
curls in my coffee cup —
real eye-opener

~ Ann Howells

pigeons preen
on the steeple
Sunday dress

~ Joanna M. Weston

tiny cat faces
bright yellow, brown whiskers
pansies in a bunch

~ Barbara D. Lazar

Cheshire cat grin
between bare pecan branches —
the waxing moon

~ Sandra Cobb

butterflies to nectar
spring sends us outdoors
~ Anjela Villarreal Ratliff

heron
in the reeds
widening ripples
~ Joanna M. Weston

distant hill
a river carrying
the spring
~ Ramesh Anand

flowing westward
the river
the stars
~ Mark E. Brager

pulling well water
alone in morning's corner
small thoughts come
~ Cara Fox

on the pool bottom
a bluebellied lizard
face toward the stars

~ Joy Acey

it is easier
to hold the sky
than the first dragonfly

~ Ed Bremson

but what do they do
my son asks of the mountains
just watch, I reply
~ Christine Boldt

Taos mountain breathes
sacred pueblo stories —
spirits rise and sigh
~ Jan Spence

mist climbs the mountains
the enlightened poet flows
wordlessly uphill
~ Aletha Irby

thermals rising
all across the valley
prayers for rain
~ Julie Bloss Kelsey

rainy season
the mountain trail
lost in the clouds
~ Mel Goldberg

prickly pear salad
nopales skinned and shredded —
thornless spring

~ Katherine Durham Oldmixon

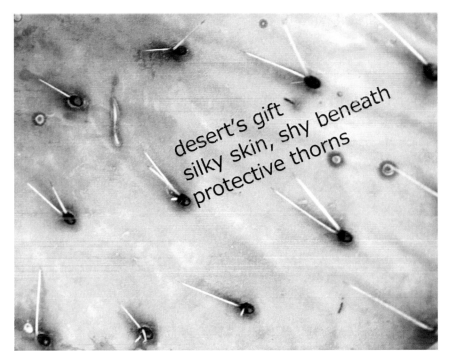

desert's gift
silky skin, shy beneath
protective thorns

~ Allene Rasmussen Nichols

desert rain
your letter arrives
and I quench my thirst

~ Richard Wells

moon rises,
shadows darken
javelinas in a line

~ Joseph Stack

honky-tonk moon . . .
her fingers trace the rim
of his Skoal ring

~ Mark E. Brager

spring gathering
the scrape of spurs
beneath the table

~ Lynn Edge

paper koi —
my kite dancing
in the winds

~ Brenda Roberts

tornado season —
against the odds
we huddle together

~ Margaret Dornaus

high noon
sunburned men scythe fields,
their feet fire-ant red

~ Margo Davis

rusty wheelbarrow
under the tall weeds

~ Geoffrey A. Landis

the dunes and I
roll over sleeplessly —
morning's lost memories

~ Brendan Egan

lifting the sky
high over Arizona
saguaro arms

~ Lesley Anne Swanson

saguaro night bloom
all these years married
to the wrong man

~ Roberta Beary

spiny arms
saguaros poke the sky
stars spill everywhere

~ Claire Vogel Camargo

swish of taffeta
in the courtyard
quinceañera

~ Lynn Edge

unearthed
Mimbres pottery shards
my flooded garden

~ Neal Whitman

WEDDING VESSEL:
TWO SIPS, TWO SOULS
NOW ONE

~ Claire Vogel Camargo

夏

Summer

sunrise
over the Sandias —
a five-balloon morning
~ Charles Trumbull

August sunflowers
heavy heads
on the weathered wall
~ Sandra D. Lynn

cicadas:
tuneless chords
scrape the sky
~ Amy Greenspan

through stardust
spilled across the Milky Way —
summer moon
~ Lesley Anne Swanson

morning glories
in an overgrown garden
twine an old tiller
~ Linda Banks

branches sway above
live oaks and sycamores —
cricket on my chest
~ Janet McCann

his wee red fan spreads
at the feeder, nearby
her shadow quivers
~ Carol Moscrip

turtle watching us
bobbing on kayak ripples
her yellow head raised
~ Lori Desrosiers

floating in the skimmer
the old grasshopper
barely struggles
~ Scott Keeney

missed by the mower
dandelions dance
in cowlicks of grass
~ Barbara Blanks

children chase monarchs
among wildflower blooms
gold dust on their hems
~ Lillian Susan Thomas

basking in sunlight
battered but still standing
this my son is joy

~ Meloni Davis

sunflowers droop
in scorching sun
old man nods his head
~ Catherine L'Herisson

grasshoppers rattle
across the caliche road
fat crows await
~ J. Todd Hawkins

starving cattle
cowboy burns spines
off cacti for feed
~ Natachia Talbert

summer showers
light little candles
on ocotillo fingers
~ Daniel Bowman

August clouds tease
floating white and thick
hoarding rain
~ J. Paul Holcomb

low clouds settle in
rain will evaporate
not precipitate

~ Allyson Whipple

dropping coins
on desert sand
monsoon rains

~ Joy Acey

summer thunder
the toad sings his aria
love near at hand

~ Peter Holland

morning drizzle
the sun follows us
into the woods

~ Máire Morrissey-Cummins

tree frogs sing
under mountain stars . . .
a dream begins

~ Sergio Ortiz

heron on stick legs,
spread wings edged by sunset —
long day, many fish

~ Joseph Hutchison

she sings
in the shower
monsoon season

~ Joan Prefontaine

dawn . . .
the mountain's reflection
trembles

~ Joanna M. Weston

tumbleweed
he tells of all the rivers
he had to cross

~ Amelia Cotter

this endless sky
I breathe in darkness
and breathe out stars

~ Lesley Anne Swanson

God pulled down the shades:
blackness at sunset
comes in clouds of dust

~ Barbara Yost

stormy night
between clouds
northern lights

~ Mel Goldberg

arroyo seco
Grandfather knew its secrets:
oceans flow beneath

~ J. Todd Hawkins

longing for canyons
red rocks and mountains —
hiking the sun, the sky

~ Stephanie Schultz

low nickers rumble
stallions on the high mesa
nubes rojas

~ Ron Blanton

the fancy dancer
kicks up a storm

~ Cliff Roberts

hikers reach
the top of the bluff
snakeweed in bloom

~ Charles Trumbull

view from the canyon rim . . .
we frame eternity with our hands

~ Amelia Cotter

76

hiking
the highest peak
I fold the map

~ Carolyn Tourney Florek

dreamcatcher
in the spider's web
a bird's feather

~ Dennis Magliozzi

Madrone reaches out
from canyon's bind —
too tight skin left behind

~ Brendan Egan

a passing cloud
catches the light of the moon —
crossing the river

~ Gary S. Rosin

high winds
the swinging shadow
of the porch light

~ Brenda Roberts

July dawn
the jogger calls roadrunner
paisano

~ Joan Prefontaine

the biplane swoops low
to feather-dust crops —
ragged ferns tremble

~ Margo Davis

where coyotes cross
skunks hesitate
Route 66

~ Ann Spiers

desert wedding
the only flower in bloom
her rose tattoo

~ Roberta Beary

sandhills — crescent dunes
    surfing
        the Permian Sea

~ Claire Vogel Camargo

bullet holes
in the trashcan —
roadside rest
~ Charlie Rossiter

cows huddle in shade
beneath a billboard ad
for the golden arches
~ Shin Yu Pai

Alamo tourists
wait in line to see what's left —
~ Nancy Fierstien

rush hour heat
listening to the radio
in someone else's car
~ Dennis Magliozzi

Rio Bravo
a girl, the hem of her dress
between borders
~ Dani Raschel Jimenez

bridal bouquet
sailing overhead
a sea of Stetsons

~ Peg Duthie

last dance
Texas two-step
lost in sawdust

~ Sue Mayfield Geiger
~ Photograph by Lisette Templin

noisy summer night
cicadas chant
meditation sounds

~ Frances Briggs

attic fan whirs
neighbor practices cello
incessantly

~ Sandra Soli

city lights —
counting constellations
to find where we are

~ Bryce Emley

daybreak —
the morning glory
bathes in dew

~ Vasile Moldovan

red fruit
from the saguaro
empty of seeds

~ Joy Acey

beyond the cattle fence
bear scat
black with berry seeds

~ Tricia Knoll

red berry
in a raven's beak —
who's the artist?

~ Wayne Lee

the
incoming
flock
thrives
off
the
dying

~ Anjela Villarreal Ratliff

collared lizard
outrunning
his shadow
    ~ Jeffrey Hoagland

                              written on the road
                              in black and white —
                              skunk's obituary
                                    ~ Sandra Cobb

off the highway, a dust storm
turning the trees formless
        ~ Rebecca Lilly

                              dust bowl
                              how many days until
                              we meet again
                                    ~ Margaret Dornaus

sun-baked by drought
the earth separates —
a dry mud puzzle
        ~ Darla McBryde

sun's heated air
weighs down the world
shadows hold their breath

~ Barbara Randals Gregg

heat shimmer . . .
a distant cross
beckons
~ Mark E. Brager

anole lizard
turns beige to bask
on sunlit mission
~ Sylvia Riojas Vaughn

prayers for shade
at the gravesite
plastic flowers
~ Sidney Bending

after cremation
her blue sari
~ Chris Ellery

scarlet hollyhocks
shield adobe mission walls —
cardinals of faith
~ Mary F. Whiteside

Ranchos de Taos radiates
summer sun, cradles moon
beneath twilight clouds

~ Jerry Hamby

sliding through fingers
many nations' beads
Four Corners
~ Doris Lynch

Delicate Arch
tourists clapping
for the echoes
~ Brad Bennett

solitude
atop an ancient mesa
endless sky
~ Barbara Randals Gregg

Morenci strip-mine
dry sweat and the taste
of copper
~ Jan Benson

graves buried in the sandstorm —
I can't remember now
what dream scared me
~ Rebecca Lilly

desert windstorm
blows sand and chisels faces —
Apache warriors
~ Diane Morinich

bright heat on sand
mica grains glisten
dancing lizard
~ Gayle Lauradunn

all things vanish here —
horned lizards, animal bones
cactus blooms
and
us

~ Allene Rasmussen Nichols

Glossary

arroyo seco – a dry creek bed, also called a wash, prone to flash flooding during heavy rains

blue norther – a swift-moving cold north wind that brings rapidly falling temperatures to the Oklahoma-Texas region

bosque – an area of sparsely treed forest that runs along stream and river banks in the Southwest

caliche – a surface soil of sand, gravel, and clay cemented together by lime deposits or calcium carbonate

Chimayo – a sanctuary and chapel north of Santa Fe, destination site for many religious pilgrimages

Delicate Arch – a 65-foot natural sandstone arch near Moab, Utah

dreamcatcher – a Native American object structured from a hoop, on which is woven a loose net (or web) decorated with feathers, beads, etc., intended to protect a person from bad dreams

fancy dance – a popular style of dance, known for athleticism and flashy colors, at Native American powwows

hoodoos – tall, thin natural columns of rock that look like spires

hornos – outdoor ovens made of adobe used by Native Americans

javelina – a mammal of the pig family that travels in small herds, also known as a peccary

Kokopelli – a Native American fertility deity and trickster often depicted as a flute player

luminarias – lanterns made of lunch-size paper bags filled with lit candles, often lining streets, sidewalks, and buildings during the Christmas season (also known as farolitos)

madrone – an evergreen with high heat tolerance, known for its exfoliating bark

Mimbres – a style of pottery with distinct geometric designs and very fine brushwork

monsoon – a subtropical ridge that produces periods of heavy rain in the Southwest in the summer

nopales – pads of prickly pear cactus from which spines have been removed, used for cooking

nubes rojas – Spanish for red skies (or red clouds)

ocotillo – a large deciduous desert shrub with spiny stems that grow up to 30 feet tall

paisano – Spanish for peasant or countryman, or in slang, a friend or pal; roadrunner

pellet stove – a stove that burns compressed wood pellets fed through a hopper to create a source of heat

piñones – the edible nutlike seeds (pine nuts) of coniferous pine trees

quinceañera – a celebration of a girl's fifteenth birthday in many Latin American cultures

ristras – colorful strings of red chile peppers bound together for drying or display

saguaro – a large tree-sized cactus of the Sonoran desert with upward-bending branches (arms)

snow-on-the-prairie – a native wildflower with white-edged green leaves and tiny white flowers

wedding vessel – a two-spouted vessel, representing husband and wife, used in traditional wedding ceremonies among the Navajo and Pueblo people

yucca – a perennial shrub with long sword-shaped leaves stemming from a woody base

Contributor Notes and Index

Joy Acey (Tucson, AZ) is a children's poet. Her poems have been published in *Highlights High Five*, *The Poetry Friday Anthology*, and many literary journals. (54, 57, 72, 82)

Gloria Amescua (Austin, TX), an inaugural member of CantoMundo, a national Latino poetry community, has many publication credits, including *di-verse-city*, *Kweli*, *Generations Literary Journal*, *Texas Poetry Calendar*, and *Acentos Review*. She has been a resident with Hedgebrook's Writers in Residence. (41, 54)

Ramesh Anand (Chennai, India) authored *Newborn Smiles*, a book of Zen poetry (Cyberwit.Net, 2012). His haiku have been translated into Japanese, German, Croatian, Serbian and Tamil; they have appeared in *Frogpond*, *Acorn*, *Magnapoets*, *Simply Haiku*, *The Heron's Nest*, *A Hundred Gourds*, and elsewhere. (56)

Evelyn Corry Appelbee (Henderson, TX), member of the Poetry Society of Texas and the National Federation of State Poetry Societies, is the author of nine books of poetry and prose. (18, 42)

Robert A. Ayres (Austin, TX) is the author of *Shadow of Wings* (Main Street Rag, 2012). His poems have appeared in *The Laurel Review*, *Marlboro Review*, *Rattle*, and *Southwestern American Literature*, among others. (37)

Linda Banks (Mesquite, TX) is a life member and past president of the Poetry Society of Texas. Intrigued by the beauty and simplicity of haiku, she recently joined the Fort Worth Haiku Society. (10, 27, 68)

Roberta Beary (Bethesda, MD) is haibun editor at *Modern Haiku*. Her book *The Unworn Necklace* (Snapshot, 2011) was a Poetry Society of America award finalist and a Haiku Society of America Merit Book Award winner. She is a three-time winner of the Tokutomi Haiku Contest. robertabeary.com (4, 62, 79)

Roy Beckemeyer (Wichita, KS) writes poetry to keep the right side of his brain as active as the left. He has recent poetry in *Coal City Review*, *The Lyric*, *Begin Again: 150 Kansas Poems*, and *200 New Mexico Poems*, among others. (28)

Sidney Bending (Victoria, BC), a member of the Haiku Society of America, has had haiku in *tinywords* and *The Wild Weathers: a gathering of love poems*. She has recent work in Arc and *Planet Earth Poetry*. (86)

Brad Bennett (Arlington, MA) has haiku in or forthcoming in *Acorn*, *bottle rockets*, *Frogpond*, *The Heron's Nest*, and *Modern Haiku*. (88)

Jan Benson (Fort Worth, TX), a member of Fort Worth Haiku Society, has recent haiku in *Small Canyons* anthologies and Baylor University's *Beall House of Poetry*. (18, 32, 88)

Barbara Blake (Marfa, TX) is the author of *A Guide to Children's Books about Asian Americans* and co-author of *Bridging Cultures: A Program Kit for Schools and Libraries*, and other references for librarians. She has over a hundred published newspaper and magazine articles to her credit. barbara-blake.com (4)

Joe Blanda (Austin, TX) is an editor and musician. A two-time Pushcart nominee, he has had poems in many local and regional publications. His songs can be heard and downloaded at: cdbaby.com/Artist/JoeBlanda. (8)

Barbara Blanks (Garland, TX), editor of *A Galaxy of Verse*, has authored three books. Recording Secretary and Librarian for the Poetry Society of Texas, she is a member of Brown Bag Poets and other poetry societies. (69)

Ron Blanton (Marietta, GA) has been writing poems for nearly twenty years. Haiku is a form he has enjoyed when working with others; he enjoys the group effort and merriment when discovering what we are capable of when we attempt this form. (38, 76)

Christine Boldt (Temple , TX) has had poems in *Christian Century*, *Windhover*, *Texas Poetry Calendar*, and elsewhere. She placed third in the Fort Worth Haiku Society's Summer 2013 contest (12, 58)

Daniel Bowman (Chapel Hill, NC) has a poem in *200 New Mexico Poems*, an online anthology celebrating New Mexico's centennial. He writes with Friday Fictioneers, an online writer's group dedicated to flash fiction. (70)

Dayna Bradley (McKinney, TX) teaches grammar, writing, and literature to home-schooled children. Living on a small family farm, she has been writing for many years and tries to submit when time allows. (14)

Ed Bremson (Raleigh, NC), founder of Mijikai Haiku group on Facebook, has been writing and publishing poetry for more than forty years. His poems have appeared in the *Longlist Anthology* of the 2011 Montreal Prize, *Wisconsin Review*, *Luna Negra*, and elsewhere. He edited *The Best of Mijikai Haiku 2012*. (57)

Mark E. Brager (Columbia, MD) has had poems in *Acorn*, *Modern Haiku*, *DailyHaiku*, *Heron's Nest*, *Frogpond*, and other journals. His pastimes include drumming and kirtan chanting, but mostly he just wants to figure out which word comes next. (6, 18, 38, 56, 60, 86)

Frances Briggs (Lago Vista, TX) believes poetry can teach, touch, and inspire. She has poems in or forthcoming in *Texas Poetry Calendar*, *Red River Review*, and *Illya's Honey*. This is her first experience with writing haiku. (6, 82)

Mike Burwell (Santa Fe, NM) has had poetry in *The Abiko Quarterly*, *Alaska Quarterly Review*, *The Pacific Review*, *The Louisville Review*, *200 New Mexico Poems*, and elsewhere. Founder of the journal *Cirque*, he has a full-length poetry collection, *Cartography of Water* (NorthShore, 2007). (37)

Claire Vogel Camargo (Austin, TX) nurtures her poetry via Austin Poetry Society, Austin International Poetry Festival, and the Writers' League of Texas. Her work has appeared in *di-verse-city*, *The Enigmatist*, *Blue Hole*, *Best Austin Poetry*, and elsewhere. (62, 63, 79)

Jesse Castro (Cibolo, TX) is a poet, outsider artist, community activist, art educator and advocate for the displaced and at-risk. He is one of the founders of National Poetry Month in San Antonio. (52)

Danny Clark (Houston, TX) is a mixed media artist. His fine art photography is oftentimes serene and minimal while his aerosol and acrylic pieces generally speak of a vibrant inner peace. dannyclarkart.com (39)

Sally Clark (Fredericksburg, TX) has had poems in *Texas Poetry Calendar*, *Chrysalis Reader*, *The Binnacle*, *Windhover*, and elsewhere. Her work can be found in gift books and anthologies from Tyndale House, Chronicle Books, Center Street Press, DaySpring Cards, and others. sallyclark.info (8, 43)

Sandra Cobb (Georgetown, TX) has served as Critique Chair and President of the Rockport Writers Group. She was a finalist in Palettes & Quills' first chapbook contest. Her haiku here are the first work she has submitted since her husband's death in 2010. (13, 34, 55, 84)

Amelia Cotter (Chicago, IL) is the author of *Maryland Ghosts: Paranormal Encounters in the Free State* and *This House: The True Story of a Girl and a Ghost*. She enjoys parallel writing lives as a haiku poet, a translator (English–German), and a technical writer. (74, 76)

Carolyn Dahl (Houston, TX) has had work in *Hawaii Review*, *Camas*, *Copper Nickel*, *Women and Poetry: Tips on Writing, Teaching and Publishing*, and elsewhere. Inspired by a trip to Japan, she created a series of Asian-influenced fiber art works using Japanese dye and printing techniques. carolyndahlstudio.com (32)

Margo Davis (Houston, TX) has poetry in or forthcoming from *New Orleans Review*, *Maple Leaf Rag*, *Passages North*, *The Louisville Review*, *Negative Capability*, *Louisiana Literature*, *The Midwest Quarterly Review*, *The Sow's Ear Poetry Review*, and other publications. (61, 78)

Meloni Davis (Houston, TX) has more time for writing and photography now that her children are grown. She enjoys traveling to new places to take photographs, she also enjoys attending meditation retreats, where the silence inspires her writing. (40, 43, 69)

Jane DeJonghe (Conifer, CO) writes high country haiku from a mountain cabin near the Mt. Evans Wilderness Area. Though new to haiku, she has been a lifelong journal writer and writes occasional articles for magazines and newspapers. She enjoys composing haiku on her daily nature walks. (4, 12, 25)

Lori Desrosiers (Westfield, MA) has a full-length book of poems, *The Philosopher's Daughter* (Salmon Poetry, 2013), and a chapbook, *Three Vanities* (Pudding House, 2009). She has had work in *Concise Delights*, *Pirene's Fountain*, and elsewhere. Editor of *Naugatuck*

River Review, Lori has an exercise in *Wingbeats: Exercises and Practice in Poetry*. (40, 68)

Margaret Dornaus (Ozark, AR) has received awards for her haiku from several international contests; her work has been published in numerous print and online journals. She is the 2011 winner of the Tanka Society of America's International Tanka Contest. (9, 12, 34, 36, 48, 60, 84)

Shannon Dougherty (Corpus Christi, TX) has degrees in English and creative writing from Texas universities. Her work has appeared in *Modern Haiku*. (3, 14, 29, 52)

Peg Duthie (Nashville, TN) is the author of *Measured Extravagance* (Upper Rubber Boot, 2012). Her poems have appeared in *tinywords, unFold, moonset, microcosms, Dwarf Stars, Texas Poetry Calendar,* and elsewhere. NashPanache.com (15, 20, 81)

Lynn Edge (Tivoli, TX) enjoys writing haibun and haiku. Her haibun have appeared in *Modern Haiku, Frogpond,* and many other journals. (32, 60, 62)

Brendan Egan (Midland, TX) is Instructor of English and Creative Writing at Midland College. His poetry and prose have appeared in *Threepenny Review, Crab Orchard Review,* and *The Georgetown Review,* among others. (61, 77)

Chris Ellery (San Angelo, TX), author of *The Big Mosque of Mercy* and two other poetry collections, has many publication credits, including *descant, Tar River Review,* and *Cimarron Review*. Co-translator of *Whatever Happened to Antara,* by award-winning Syrian author Walid Ikhlassi, Chris teaches poetry and poetry writing at Angelo State University. (10, 86)

Bryce Emley (Gallup, NM) has edited numerous journals, including *The Florida Review, H_NGM_N,* and *12:51*. His work can be found in *Modern Haiku, The Pinch, Hawaii Review, Yemassee, Orange Quarterly Review, Pleiades,* and other publications. (82)

Robert Epstein (El Cerrito, CA) is a haiku poet/editor. His latest book is *Checkout Time Is Noon: Death Awareness Haiku*. (Wasteland, 2012). (6, 12, 38, 50)

Nancy Fierstien (Dripping Springs, TX) is the editor of *Best Austin Poetry*, 2010-11 and 2011-12. She has had poetry in *di-verse-city* and *Bigger Than They Appear,* an anthology of very short poems (Accents, 2011). Nancy hosts Thirsty Thursday, a monthly venue for poets, musicians, and storytellers. (80)

Gretchen Fletcher (Ft. Lauderdale, FL) leads poetry and essay workshops for Florida Center for the Book and mentors fifth-grade poets. She has won the Poetry Society of America's Bright Lights, Big Verse competition and other awards. A Pushcart nominee, Gretchen is the author of two chapbooks, *That Severed Cord* and *The Scent of Oranges*. (26, 31, 48)

Carolyn Tourney Florek (Houston, TX), poet and visual artist, has had poems in *The Texas Review, Illya's Honey,* and elsewhere. A Pushcart nominee, she is co-founder, with her husband Bob, of Mutabilis Press, a non-profit literary press devoted to poetry. (42, 77)

Sue Foster (Cypress, TX) has recent poetry in the *Texas Poetry Calendar*. She hopes to continue learning and growing every day. (6)

Cara Fox (Hondo Mesa, NM), a freelance writer, has had poems in *Animus, The Dunes Review, Stuff Magazine, The Aurorean, Puckerbrush Review, The Café Review, Stolen Island, Venus Envy,* and *200 New Mexico Poems,* as well as other publications. (42, 56)

Susan Gabrielle (Penn Valley, CA) has work in or forthcoming from *The Christian Science Monitor, Baltimore Review, Heyday, Sugar Mule,* and elsewhere. A Pushcart nominee, as well as a finalist in the Tiny Lights Narrative Essay Contest, Susan works as an editor and teaches writing and literature classes. (34)

Alan Gann (Plano, TX) is a long-time workshopper with the Dallas Poets Community; he helps edit their literary journal, *Illya's Honey*. Alan's poetry has appeared in *Borderlands, North Texas Review, San Pedro River Review,* and elsewhere. He has been nominated for the Pushcart Prize and Best of the Net. (42)

Sue Mayfield Geiger (Bacliff, TX), a freelance writer, has recent literary work in *The Binnacle, The Write Place at the Write Time, Inner Landscapes,* and other publications. *Gibbons Street* (2011) is her first book of verse and prose. smgwriter.com (81)

Mel Goldberg (Ajijic, Mexico) taught high school and college literature and writing in

California, Illinois, Arizona, and England. He is the author of *A Few Berries from the Tree*, a book of haiku, as well as two books of poetry and photography, *The Cyclic Path* and *Sedona Poems*. (36, 58, 74)

Katie Goode (Austin, TX) is a photographer and nurse who always keeps an eye out for beautiful trees and nice bistros. (53)

Amy L. Greenspan (Austin, TX) is the author of several employment law books. Her poems have appeared in *Texas Poetry Calendar*, *di-verse-city*, Story Circle Network's *True Words Anthology*, *Story Circle Journal*, and *The Ghazal Page*. (13, 14, 67)

Barbara Randals Gregg (Austin, TX) has poetry in *di-verse-city*, *Blue Hole*, *The Austin Poetry Society Annual*, *Texas Poetry Calendar*, and *Wingbeats: Exercises and Practice in Poetry* (Dos Gatos Press, 2011). (85, 88)

Jerry Hamby (Houston, TX) is the author of *Letters Drawn in Water* (Pecan Grove, 2004). He has poetry in several journals, including *Concho River Review*, *Palo Alto Review*, *New Texas*, and *Windhover*. Jerry has twice won the Conference of College Teachers of English Creative Writing Award, and he was a Featured Poet at Houston Poetry Fest 2011. (7, 87)

Jerri Hardesty (Brierfield, AL) and husband, Kirk, also a poet, run NewDawnUnlimited, Inc., host of the BamaSlam Montevallo Poetry Slam in Montevallo, AL, and other poetry events. Jerri has had over 250 poems published, and has won more than 500 awards and titles in both written and spoken word/performance poetry. (19)

Lisa Hase-Jackson (Albuquerque, NM) is editor of *200 New Mexico Poems*, a New Mexico Centennial Project. She has recent work in *Sugar Mule* and *To the Stars Through Difficulty*, a Kansas renga project and print anthology. Lisa manages the blog, ZingaraPoet.net, featuring original poetry, interviews, writing exercises, and poetry prompts. (6, 37)

J. Todd Hawkins (Crowley, TX) has had poems in *American Literary Review*, *Antietam Review*, *Westview*, *Wisconsin Review*, *Borderlands*, and elsewhere. He has served as co-editor for *di-verse-city* and recently presented a series of poems at the Oklahoma State University Humanities Conference in Stillwater. (26, 70, 75)

Jeff Hoagland (Hopewell, NJ) enjoys visiting and exploring the Southwest. For him harvesting haiku is a spiritual act that keeps him aware, appreciative, and connected. Jeff's haiku can be found in *Modern Haiku*, *The Heron's Nest*, *Frogpond*, *bottle rockets*, and elsewhere. He was featured in *A New Resonance 7*, an anthology of emerging voices in haiku. (84)

J. Paul Holcomb (Double Oak, TX), past president of the Poetry Society of Texas, is current president of the Poets of Tarrant County. He is the author of *Looking for Love in the Telecom Corridor*, a book of poems; *Love, or Something Like It*, a chapbook; and *Story Texas*, a mini-chapbook. His poems have appeared in *Texas Poetry Calendar* and elsewhere. (70)

Peter Holland (San Antonio, TX) is a lifelong San Antonian. The beauty of the land and its history are an endless wellspring for his inspired pen. He shares his love of the place and of words at several local open mike events in and around the city he so loves. (28, 72)

Ann Howells (Carrollton, TX) has two chapbooks, *Black Crow in Flight* (Main Street Rag, 2007) and *The Rosebud Diaries* (Willet, 2012). Twice nominated both for a Pushcart and Best of the Net, she has poems in *Borderlands*, *San Pedro River Review*, *Spillway*, and elsewhere. Anne has served as editor of *Illya's Honey* for fourteen years. (16, 26, 55)

Joseph Hutchison (Indian Hills, CO) is the author of thirteen books of poetry, including *Thread of the Real* (Conundrum, 2012); a chapbook, *The Earth-Boat* (Folded Word, 2012); and *Marked Men*, three long poems (Turning Point, forthcoming). jhwriter.com (41, 72)

Cindy Huyser (Austin, TX) has had poems in a number of journals and anthologies, including *The Comstock Review*, *Borderlands*, and *Layers*. She is lead editor of the *Texas Poetry Calendar*. (30, 31, 50)

Aletha Irby (Austin, TX) is grateful to have been granted this time, on this planet, to spend with the English language. (10, 20, 58)

Elizabeth Jacobson (Santa Fe, NM) is the author of the poetry collection *Her Knees Pulled In* (Tres Chicas, 2012), as well as a chapbook, *Four Hot Days* (Turtle Path, 2001). Recipient of the Jim Sagel prize for poetry, she has taught writing in New York City and in Santa Fe. (36)

Dani Raschel Jimenez (Laredo, TX) has visited other states, but she can't imagine calling anywhere but Texas home. If you ever find yourself in Laredo, look her up. She just might treat you to a Corona. (80)

Marcelle Kasprowicz (Austin, TX) writes in English and French. She is the author of two poetry collections, *Organza Skies: Poems from the Davis Mountains* (2005) and *Children Playing with Leopards* (2012). (36, 52)

Scott Keeney (Newtown, CT) has had work in *Columbia Poetry Review, Court Green, Failbetter, Mudlark, Poetry East,* and elsewhere. He is the author of *Sappho Does Hay(na) ku,* a limited edition (Sephyrus, 2008). (68)

Larry Kelly (Houston, TX) enjoys Chinese calligraphy. He plays bass fiddle and enjoys singing classic country music and bluegrass. Writing poetry is not a choice for him; it comes unbidden. He has poems in *Texas Poetry Calendar* and *Blue Hole.* (29, 39)

Julie Bloss Kelsey (Germantown, MD) rediscovered her love of short-form poetry after the birth of her third child in 2009. She has poems in *Scifaikuest, Notes from the Gean,* and *The Heron's Nest,* among others. One of her scifaiku (science fiction haiku) won the 2011 Dwarf Stars Award. starsinmysugarbowl.blogspot.com (58)

Tricia Knoll (Portland, OR) has a daily haiku practice. She travels each year to Arizona and New Mexico—to study poetry, to write, to walk. Recent poetry publications include *RAIN Magazine, Muddy River Poetry Review, VoiceCatcher,* and *Verseweaver.* (83)

Geoffrey A. Landis (Berea, OH) is a science fiction writer, a scientist, and a poet. He is the author of the poetry collection *Iron Angels* (vanZeno, 2009). geoffreylandis.com (18, 36, 61)

Albert Vetere Lannon (Tucson, AZ), poetry writer and performer for more than sixty years, recently won first prize in poetry from the Society of Southwestern Authors. Albert has published several chapbooks and two works of history; he chronicles local news for his Picture Rocks community. (35, 53)

Gayle Lauradunn (Albuquerque, NM) has had poems in *Puerto del Sol, Adobe Walls,* 200 *New Mexico Poems, Tsunami,* and others, including a series of haiku in *Small Canyons.* Recently, she participated in Giving Voice to Image, a collaborative poetry and art show at Vivo Contemporary Gallery in Santa Fe. (89)

Barbara D. Lazar (San Antonio, TX) is the author of *Pillow Book of the Flower Samurai,* a historical novel set in 12th-century Japan that includes more than forty tanka. Her poetry, including haiku and tanka, has appeared in *The Aurorean, Dreamcatcher,* and elsewhere. Barbara teaches poetry classes in San Antonio. barbaralazar.com (55)

Wayne Lee (Santa Fe, NM) has had poems in *Tupelo Press, The New Guard, Slipstream, The Floating Bridge Anthology, Conversations Across Borders,* and other publications. He won the 2012 Mark Fischer Poetry Prize. A Pushcart and Best of the Net nominee, Wayne has a third collection of poems in search of a publisher. wayneleepoet.com (16, 83)

Catherine L'Herisson (Garland, TX), Life Member and current vice president of the Poetry Society of Texas, has had poems in the Poetry Society of Texas *Book of the Year* and *Encore,* the anthology of the National Federation of State Poetry Societies. Her poems have also appeared in *Lucidity, Peace Words, Windhover,* and other publications. (50, 70)

Becky Liestman (Shorewood, MN) published her first haiku in a Minneapolis journal of best K-12 writing. A former resident of the Writer's Room in New York City, she has had poems in *The Enigmatist, di-verse-city,* and other publications. Becky has read at the Weisman Art Museum in Minneapolis, the Dodge Poetry Festival in Newark, and elsewhere. (21, 29)

Rebecca Lilly (Port Republic, VA) has several collections of poems, including two books of haiku, *Yesterday's Footprints* (Red Moon, 2012), and *A Prism of Wings* (Antrim, 2013). (37, 38, 84, 88)

Ellaraine Lockie (Sunnyvale, CA) has received numerous awards, including the Women's National Book Association's Poetry Prize. Poetry Editor for *Lilipoh,* she has a new chapbook, *Coffee House Confessions* (Silver Birch). Ellaraine has an exercise in *Wingbeats: Exercises and Practice in Poetry* (Dos Gatos Press, 2011). (14, 40, 52)

Doris Lynch (Bloomington, IN) spent three months in Taos; she loves visiting the Zion National Park and Bryce Canyon areas of Utah. Her haiku have appeared in *Frogpond, Modern Haiku,* and *Lynx.* She has longer poems in numerous journals. (8, 12, 26, 33, 88)

Sandra D. Lynn (Albuquerque, NM) is the author of *I Must Hold These Strangers* (Prickly Pear, 1980) and *Where Rainbows Wait for Rain: The Big Bend Country,* with Richard Fenker (Tangram, 1989). She is a recipient of the Dobie Paisano Fellowship. (3, 16, 53, 67)

Dennis Magliozzi (Dover, NH), writer and teacher, is pursuing an MFA in Poetry with Vermont College of Fine Arts. (14, 77, 80)

Wade Martin (Austin, TX) has recent poems in *Red River Review* and *Front Porch Journal.* (53)

Darla McBryde (Spring, TX) is a member of Gulf Coast Poets, the Austin Poetry Society, and the Poetry Society of Texas. She has work in or forthcoming from *Illya's Honey, Cenizo Journal,* and *200 New Mexico Poems.* Darla has published six chapbooks, most recently *Thorns Against the Sky* and *Querencia.* (30, 54, 84)

Janet McCann (College Station, TX) has had poems in *Kansas Quarterly, Parnassus, Nimrod, Sou'wester,* and elsewhere. Her most recent poetry collection is *Emily's Dress* (Pecan Grove, 2004). A 1989 NEA Creative Writing Fellowship winner, she is the author of *Wallace Stevens Revisited: "The Celestial Possible."* (68)

Kaitlin Mara Meadows (Tucson, AZ) has six poetry chapbooks, including *The Indigo Kimono.* She has incorporated her latest group of poems into *Clairvoyance,* a handmade, hand-painted book. Kaitlin is a member of Paper Works, the Sonoran Collective of Book and Paper Artists. kaitlinmeadows.com (35)

Teresa Milbrodt (Gunnison, CO) is the author of *Bearded Women: Stories* (ChiZine, 2011). She has many publication credits, including *North American Review, Crazyhorse, Indiana Review,* and *Nimrod.* A Pushcart nominee, Teresa is an Assistant Professor of Creative Writing at Western State Colorado University. (48)

Vasile Moldovan (Bucharest, Romania) was chairman of the Romanian Society of Haiku, 2001–09. He is the author of several books of haiku—*Via Dolorosa* (1998), *The Moon's Unseen Face* (2001), *Noah's Ark* (2001), *Ikebana* (2005) and *On a Summer Day* (2010). (15, 25, 82)

Diane Morinich (Bridgeport, PA), member of a Facebook haiku group, is co-author, with Pete Reitano, of *The Life and Times of a Nobody.* A member of Art4Good, she contributed to *ART and Time,* published for charitable support, and to *Mashup,* a poetry and art jam published by Blurb, also for charitable support. (89)

Máire Morrissey-Cummins (Greystones, Ireland) enjoys writing and painting (watercolor). She has work in *Bamboo Dreams: An Anthology of Haiku Poetry from Ireland* (Doghouse, 2012). (3, 28, 38, 40, 47, 72)

Carol Moscrip (San Diego, CA), a life-long poet and writing teacher, has had poems in *Malpais Review, Adobe Walls, La Llorona,* and elsewhere. She is the author of one full-length book of poetry, *Straw,* and four chapbooks. (68)

Allene Rasmussen Nichols (Dallas, TX) has had poems in *Naugatuck River Review, Hinchas de Poesía, New Plains Review, Dance the Guns to Silence: 100 Poems for Ken Saro-Wiwa,* and other publications. Her plays have been produced in Dallas, New York, and California. allenen.wordpress.com (59, 89)

Miranda Nicole (San Antonio, TX) enjoys hiking, strange nooks to read, folding laundry, cat naps, massive dogs, shag coats, and Netflix. When she walks into the mountains, sometimes she forgets to come back out. (28)

Katherine Durham Oldmixon (Austin, TX) is the author of the poetry chapbook *Water Signs* (Finishing Line, 2009). She teaches creative writing and literature at historic Huston-Tillotson University in Austin, TX, and in the low-residency MFA program at the University of New Orleans. (59)

Sergio Ortiz (San Juan, Puerto Rico) has a recent poetry chapbook, *Bedbugs in My Mattress* (Flutter, 2010). His photographic chapbook is *The Sugarcane Harvest* (Avantacular, 2010). Sergio has work in or forthcoming from *Shot Glass Journal* and elsewhere. He is a Pushcart and Best of the Net nominee. (17, 18, 72)

Stephen Page (Buenos Aires, Argentina) is the author of *The Timbre of Sand* and *Still Dan-*

delions. Recipient of the Jess Cloud Memorial Prize for Poetry, he has an MFA from Bennington College. (10)

Shin Yu Pai (Seattle, WA) is the author of *Adamantine* (White Pine, 2010), *Sightings* (1913 Press, 2007), and *Equivalence* (La Alameda, 2003), as well as a number of smaller letterpress, limited edition projects. Her work has appeared in *Spoon River Poetry Review, Columbia Poetry Review, Magnolia,* and elsewhere. shinyupai.com (80)

Christa Pandey (Austin, TX) has had an interest in photography since childhood. Recently, she learned the art of combining her love of words with her love of images. (51)

Pearl Pirie (Ottawa, ON) has been writing Eastern forms for several years; her poetry collection *been shed bore* (Chaudiere, 2010) includes a few. A member of Tanka Canada, Haiku Canada, and Kado Ottawa, Pearl has senryu in *Lighting the Global Lantern: A Teacher's Guide to Writing Haiku and Related Literary Forms.* (27)

Barbara Green Powell (Beaumont, TX) has memberships in the Poetry Society of Texas (PST) and the National Poetry Society. Her poems have appeared in the PST *Book of the Year, Texas Poetry Calendar, Voices Along the River,* and elsewhere. Barbara enjoys introducing poetry to school-age children. (33)

Joan Prefontaine (Cottonwood, AZ) has worked as a teacher, editor and nature writer for magazines. She has haiku in or forthcoming from *tinywords, Modern Haiku,* and *Frogpond.* Some of her longer poems have been set to music by contemporary composers. (11, 17, 30, 47, 73, 78)

Anjela Villarreal Ratliff (Austin, TX) is the author of several poetry chapbooks. Her poem "I Exist" was animated by Francesca Talenti for the 2001 Poetry in Motion project for KLRU TV. Three of her haiku have been selected for Poetry with Wheels—for display on Capital Metro busses in Austin. (56, 83)

John E. Rice (Houston, TX) has work in *TEXAS Magazine, Texas Poetry Calendar,* and other publications. His artwork is in several private collections around the world. (19, 43)

Brenda Roberts (Fort Worth, TX), co-founder of the Fort Worth Haiku Society and current secretary, is a writer of fantasy, fiction, romance, short stories, and poetry. Widely anthologized, she is the author of *A Cold North Wind,* a fantasy fiction series. (19, 40, 60, 78)

Cliff Roberts (Fort Worth , TX), founder and current president of the Fort Worth Haiku Society, started tinkering around with haiku in high school. His haiku can be found at *Simply Haiku* and elsewhere. (19, 32, 49, 50, 76)

Gary S. Rosin (Houston, TX) has poems and short stories in or forthcoming from *Concho River Review, Crosscurrents, New Texas, Sulphur River Literary Review,* and other publications. His chapbook *Standing Inside the Web* won the 1990 Lucidity Chapbook Contest. Gary is Program Chair of the Houston Poetry Fest. 4p.creations.com (78)

Charlie Rossiter (Oak Park, IL), NEA Fellowship recipient and four-time Pushcart Prize nominee, hosts poetrypoetry.com. He has four books of poetry; with Jeffrey Winke, he co-edited *Third Coast Haiku Anthology.* His work has been featured on NPR and at the Dodge Poetry Festival. (3, 33, 80)

Stephanie Schultz (Saint Paul, MN) is a poet, marathon runner, and MFA student. Her work has appeared in *Paddlefish* and at tcmevents.org (76)

Jennifer Smith (Los Angeles, CA) has been published in *Zocalo Public Square* and the anthologies *Love Notes* and *Beatrice Emerges.* Her favorite poet is Rilke; T.S. Eliot is a close second. (8, 42)

Sandra Soli (Edmond, OK) has recent poetry, short fiction, or photography in *Ruminate, Parody, Crosstimbers, Sugar Mule, Cybersoleil, Oklahoma Today,* and elsewhere. Her honors include an Oklahoma Book Award, the Eyster Poetry Prize from *New Delta Review,* a nomination for AWP's Intro Award, and two nominations for the Pushcart Prize. (82)

Jan Spence (Denton, TX) has work in or forthcoming from *Texas Poetry Calendar, Red River Review,* and *The Senior Voice,* among others. She is a participant in Merging Visions, a collaborative exhibit of art and poetry sponsored by the Denton Poets' Assembly and the

Visual Arts Society of Texas. Jan's chapbook is *Navigating the Old Road.* (58)

Ann Spiers (Vashon Island, WA), a Haiku Northwest member, has haiku in *Mayfly, Modern Haiku, The Heron's Nest,* and elsewhere. She helps calligrapher Kaj Wyn Berry with Vashon Island's Hiway Haiku, a series of roadside placards featuring haiku. Ann attends Mondays at Three, a haiku sharing group that has met monthly for fifteen years. (54, 78)

Joseph Stack (Cottonwood, AZ) has been intrigued by and dabbled in haiku over the years. Having moved from the Pacific Northwest to Arizona, he is awestruck by the stark beauty of the Southwestern landscape. (34, 60)

Sandi Stromberg (Houston, TX) has had poems in *TimeSlice, The Weight of Addition, Improbable Worlds, Illya's Honey,* and *Sol Magazine,* among others. A Pushcart nominee, she has been a juried poet at the Houston Poetry Fest six times. (34)

Susan Beall Summers (Hutto, TX) has had poems in many publications, including *diverse-city, Poetry in the First* (Chicago Poetry Press), and *Awesmic City Austin Texas Day 12.12.12.* Her poetry collection is *Friends, Sins & Possibilities.* tidalpoolpoet.com (16, 32, 54)

Sheri Sutton (Wichita Falls, TX) retired in August 2009 to pursue a writing career. She has had work in *Wichita Falls Literature and Art Review, A Book of the Year* (Poetry Society of Texas), *The Secret Place,* and elsewhere. Sheri is a member of the Wichita Falls Poetry Society and the Poetry Society of Texas. (47)

Lesley Anne Swanson (Coopersburg, PA) is enamored of Japanese short-form poetry, especially tanka and haiku; she has been published in numerous poetry journals. (4, 13, 47, 62, 67, 74)

Natachia Talbert (China Spring, TX) has always had a passion to write short stories, poetry, and haiku. She lives on a working cattle ranch—a wonderful slice of nature and beauty, a great setting for creating. (70)

Lisette Templin (Seabrook, TX) practiced architecture before becoming a photographer. She found that many of the same issues that attracted her to architecture also drew her to photography, namely the pursuit of a sense of timelessness and a fascination with light and shadow. (81)

Lillian Susan Thomas (Houston, TX) has been writing poetry for more than forty-five years. Twice a juried poet at the Houston Poetry Fest, she has had poems in *Trinity Review, The Bayou Review, di-verse-city, River City Free Press,* and other publications. (7, 48, 69)

Charles Trumbull (Santa Fe, NM) is a past president of the Haiku Society of America. Since 2006 he has been the editor of *Modern Haiku.* Charles is currently secretary of the New Mexico State Poetry Society. His haiku chapbook, *Between the Chimes,* was published in 2011. (8, 26, 50, 51, 67, 76)

Sylvia Riojas Vaughn (Plano, TX) has a poem on San Antonio's VIA Metropolitan Transit vehicles as part of Poetry on the Move, celebrating National Poetry Month, April 2013. A Pushcart nominee, she has had poems in *Illya's Honey, Elegant Rage: A Poetic Tribute to Woody Guthrie,* and elsewhere. (15, 86)

Loretta Diane Walker (Odessa, TX) won the 2011 Bluelight Press Book Award for *Word Ghetto,* her second book of poems. A Pushcart nominee, she has multiple publication credits, including *Concho River Review, Red River Review,* and *From Under the Bridges of America: Homeless Poetry Anthology.* (16)

Richard Wells (Seattle, WA) is a community organizer and poet who lives in the Pacific Northwest with his wife Reggie Bardach, and their good dog Sam. He left his heart in Santa Fe many years ago. (25, 59)

Christine Wenk-Harrison (Lago Vista, TX) grew up in New Mexico and Texas, where her mother introduced her to haiku. She has had poems in *Texas Poetry Calendar, The Enigmatist, Blue Hole, Illya's Honey, Elegant Rage,* and *Red River Review.* (5, 30, 33, 49)

Joanna M. Weston (Shawnigan Lake, BC) is the author a poetry collection, *A Summer Father* (Frontenac, 2006), as well as two books for middle readers, *Those Blue Shoes* (Clarity, 2006) and *The Willow Tree Girl* (Electric e-Book, 2003). 1960willowtree.wordpress.com (4, 28, 55, 56, 74)

Allyson Whipple (Austin, TX) has lived in Texas since 2008; its diverse landscapes inform much of her poetry. Allyson has a debut chapbook, *We're Smaller Than We Think We Are*, (Finishing Line, 2013). allysonmwhipple.wordpress.com (71)

Mary F. Whiteside (Plano, TX) is never without a notebook in her backpack; she enjoys writing about rural areas of the United States, especially the Southwest. Her work has appeared in *Contemporary Haibun Online*, *Haibun Today*, *Forces Literary Journal*, and *200 New Mexico Poems*. (5, 86)

Neal Whitman (Pacific Grove, CA) is inspired by the Southwest and the cultures that have shaped it. He has published many poems in Japanese forms—haiku, senryu, haiga, haibun, and tanka. In recital Neal loves to combine his poetry with his wife Elaine's Native American flute and her photography. (5, 31, 62)

p. wick (Empire, CO) has been a writer for more than forty years. He resides in the realm of the Snow and Thunder Deities, the central Rocky Mountains of Colorado. (10, 30, 52)

James Willard (Baytown, TX) is a graduate of the San Francisco Art Institute, a painter who enjoys writing as well. His most recent painting show was at the Jung Center of Houston. (27, 48)

Barbara Yost (Phoenix, AZ), a newspaper feature writer for many years, currently works as a freelance newspaper, magazine, and fiction writer. She has a master's degree in English and an MFA in creative writing, both from Arizona State University. (74)

Editors

Scott Wiggerman (Austin, TX) is the author of two books of poetry, *Presence* and *Vegetables and Other Relationships*, as well as the editor of several volumes, including *Wingbeats: Exercises & Practice in Poetry* and *Big Land, Big Sky, Big Hair*. He has published widely—from journals such as *Comstock Review*, *Spillway*, *Southwestern American Literature*, *Switched-on Gutenberg*, and *Hobble Creek Review* (which has twice nominated him for a Pushcart); to anthologies such as *City of the Big Shoulders*, *Among the Leaves*, *Two Southwests*, *Collecting Life*, and *This New Breed*; to nonfiction texts such as *Poetry as Spiritual Practice*, *The Book of Forms*, and *Poem, Revised*. A popular instructor of poetry workshops, Scott is chief editor for Dos Gatos Press, publisher of the *Texas Poetry Calendar*, now in its sixteenth year. http://swig.tripod.com (21)

Constance Campbell (Henderson, TN) is a poet, editor, and playwright. Her haiku, tanka, and other short poems have been published in *Lilliput Review*, *The Texas Observer*, *Borderlands*, *Moonbathing*, and online at *One Hundred Gourds*. In 2011, one of her haiku won first prize in the Medizen Micropoetry Competition, sponsored by the London-based visual artist/micropoet Juliea Stewart. Constance is very proud to have had this poem hanging in an art gallery in Japan as part of a collaborative work by Stewart. In 2004, Constance edited and published the poetry collection, *WILD PLUM*, which featured poets from Austin, TX, along with notables from other areas of the U.S. and overseas. As a playwright, she had two children's plays produced in Austin, one of which was written while playwright-in-residence at St. Edward's University. (21)

Foreword

Penny Harter is published widely in journals and anthologies; her literary autobiography appears in *Contemporary Authors*. Penny's more recent collections include *One Bowl* (e-chapbook of haibun, 2012); *Recycling Starlight*, (2010); an illustrated children's alphabestiary, *The Beastie Book* (2010); *The Night Marsh* (2008); *Along River Road* (2005); and *Buried in the Sky* (2002). An earlier collection, *Lizard Light: Poems from the Earth* (1998), contains many poems written while living in Santa Fe, NM. With her late husband, William J. (Bill) Higginson, Penny co-authored *The Haiku Handbook* (25th Anniversary Edition, 2010). Among her collections that feature haiku is the now out-of-print *Stages and Views*, poems based on the woodblock prints of Hiroshige and Hokusai (Katydid Books, 1994). A new collection of haibun and free verse, *The Great Blue*, is forthcoming from Mountains and Rivers Press. 2hweb.net/penhart (vii)